CW01670016

Comfort and Consolation

Prayers for funerals and the bereaved

David Adam
Nick Fawcett
Susan Hardwick
Susan Sayers
Ray Simpson

kevin
mayhew

kevin mayhew

First published in Great Britain in 2011 by Kevin Mayhew Ltd
Buxhall, Stowmarket, Suffolk IP14 3BW
Tel: +44 (0) 1449 737978 Fax: +44 (0) 1449 737834
E-mail: info@kevinmayhewltd.com

www.kevinmayhew.com

ISBN 978 1 84867 346 5
Catalogue No. 1501263

Cover design by Rob Mortonson
© Image used under licence from Shutterstock Inc.
Typeset by Rob Mortonson

Printed and bound in Great Britain

Contents

Private Prayers

Foreword

Death is a public as well as a private event.

The loss of a loved one, companion, friend is of course very personal, evoking deep and varied emotions. But it is also an event that stretches beyond the immediate family and friends and at a funeral or memorial service it takes on a public aspect.

In this public setting the words that are spoken tend to be quite formal, holding together some sense of order amid the chaos of private loss, as well as giving voice to the thanks for a life well lived. The words seek to convey both the feelings that it might be difficult for individuals to express in such a setting and also the comfort and consolation that the story of faith and the tradition of religious belief offer to those who are bereaved. Such words are not simply plasters to smother the wounds of loss but are there to express the reality of grief and pain, while also speaking of comfort and hope that goes beyond this moment and beyond ourselves. The funeral, as a public event, is therefore a very important and significant point in a person's and community's time of grief. It gives public expression to what is deeply personal.

While a funeral will often have personal tributes to the one who has died and family members may express their thanks and their loss, it is not usually the occasion for expressing those deeply felt personal agonies of guilt and loss, despair and anger that can haunt the grief of an individual. Yet these powerful and disturbing feelings also need expressing and it is most likely that, if done at all, it will be in private.

This book seeks to provide appropriate words for both public and private use. They do not seek to replace those liturgical forms of service provided by the various churches, but to be an additional resource which ministers and the bereaved can draw upon when planning a particular funeral. Some reflections upon death and grief in general and specific death events in particular are also offered.

In the second half of the book there are prayers that are more suitable for private use. They cannot replace an individual's own words but they may well articulate what is felt but cannot easily be expressed. Like all the prayers offered they seek to be honest to the turmoil of feelings that death evokes, especially where death is particularly traumatic. They also express the hope the Christian gospel provides amid the sadness, confusion, doubt and anger. Some texts of comfort are offered on which to reflect.

Public Prayers

At the opening of the service

1 Loving God,
we come today struggling for words to express our feelings,
lost for words to express our thanks
for all *Name* has meant to us.
We come with sorrow as we think of our loss,
with gratitude as we recall the person *Name* has been,
with praise as we remember
all you have done through *her/him*,
with faith as we commit both A and ourselves
to your eternal care.

Nick Fawcett

2 Loving God,
draw near to us as we draw near to you.
Speak to us through the words of Scripture,
through our prayers,
through all we shall share,
so that, believing in the Gospel and trusting in Christ,
we may receive the comfort, peace and strength
you long to give us,
and find hope in this life,
and the life to come.
Through Jesus Christ our Lord.

Nick Fawcett

3 God be blessed for the wonder of a life.

Jesus said: My peace I leave with you.
Let not your hearts be troubled or afraid.

The lights fade, the rumble of creation diminishes,
mists descend and blanket out what has been.
Our Creator calls us to release the one whom we love
from this world.
Our Saviour calls us to remain united with he who alone
can help the one who has left us.

Continued overleaf

Since it was you, O Christ, who bought each soul –
at the time it gave up its life, at the time of returning to clay;
at the time of the shedding of blood,
at the time of severing the breath,
at the time you delivered judgement –
may your peace be on your ingathering of souls.
Jesus Christ, Son of gentle Mary,
your peace be upon your own ingathering.

Ray Simpson

4 Lord,
someone we have loved has died,
someone special to us,
precious,
irreplaceable.
And we know there are no words we can say at this moment
to express what we are feeling,
no words that can alleviate our sorrow
or take away our pain.

So we come today simply to bring you the grief,
the shock and the pain,
the emptiness, the anger and the despair,
the loneliness, the fear and the uncertainty
which overwhelms us at this time.
We come bringing those honestly before you,
and asking for strength in this time of darkness.
Hold on to us,
even when we find it hard to hold on to you.
Be very near,
even when we feel you to be very far.
Support us in the days ahead,
and grant the comfort you have promised,
until the time finally comes when we can look back
not just with pain but thanksgiving –
not just with sorrow but with joy.
Through Jesus Christ our Lord,
the Resurrection and the Life!

Nick Fawcett

5 Eternal God,
draw near today as we worship you,
so that this time of sorrow and heartache
will also be one of joy and hope;
this day of endings also one of new beginnings;
this acknowledgement of death also a celebration of life,
lived to the full and with more yet to come.
Reach out into the pain of this moment,
giving the assurance that those who mourn will be comforted,
that your purpose continues,
and that nothing finally can ever separate us
from your love in Christ.
Help us, then,
giving thanks for what has been
and looking forward to what shall be,
to receive your peace, strength, help and love now,
through Jesus Christ our Lord.

Nick Fawcett

6 We are here to express sorrow that a life is ended,
to give thanks for a life well-lived.
We are here grieving that a life is over,
but rejoicing that life eternal has just begun.
We are here conscious of separation,
yet confident we shall meet again.
We are here remembering what has been,
and looking forward to what shall be.
We are here to pay tribute to all *Name* has meant to us,
to remind ourselves of all *she/he* means to God.
We are here to entrust someone we have greatly loved
to his eternal keeping,
and to entrust ourselves to the same God
who so greatly loves us.
Listen then to words of Scripture and tribute,
bring your pain, your shock and sadness,
offer to God this time of worship,
and receive the comfort he longs to give you,
in the name of Christ.

Nick Fawcett

7 We have come together in the presence of God,
and in the name of Christ.
We come with sorrow,
but also with hope;
to express loss,
but also to give thanks;
to recognise death,
but also to celebrate life;
to look back at all that has been,
but also to look forward to all that is yet to be.
Come then in faith, for God is here –
the God who has promised that, in life or in death,
he is with us,
the God who gives all who truly believe
the assurance of his eternal blessing.

Nick Fawcett

8 Loving God,
we come today to express our sorrow but also our joy,
to remember but also to anticipate,
to mourn but also to give thanks.
Lord, in your mercy,
hear our prayer.
We come with gratitude in our hearts
for all *Name* has meant to us,
for all *she/he* continues to mean to us,
for all *she/he* will always mean to you.
Lord, in your mercy,
hear our prayer.

We come to acknowledge a life well-lived,
and in faith to commit both *Name* and ourselves
to your eternal care.
Lord, in your mercy,
hear our prayer.

Loving God,
draw near to us as we draw near to you.
Speak to us through the words of Scripture and tribute,
through our hymns and prayers,
through all we share,
so that believing in the Good News of Christ,
and trusting in him,
we may receive the comfort he promises,
the peace that passes all understanding,
and the assurance of everlasting life,
through Jesus Christ our Lord.
Lord, in your mercy,
hear our prayer,
for in his name we pray.

Nick Fawcett

Prayers for those who mourn

9 Father God,
we pray
for those today
who are sad and upset,
who are grieving
for the ones they love.
We want to wrap
our thoughts and prayers
around them,
comfort and protect them.
Father God,
please help them to know
how much we care,
how much we feel for their loss,
for their heartache and pain,
and as we pray
our hearts
go out to them.

Tony Bower

10 Loving Lord,
as we remember what *Name* meant to us,
we pray for those who mourn
and who, in their grief, are angry with you.
Comfort and console them, please, Lord,
as your Son showed his concern and love
for those who had lost a loved one.
We know that *Name* is at peace with you now,
but help those who remain to know this
so that they can remember fondly,
but also go forward hopefully,
confident in the love of Jesus Christ.

Rupert Bristow

11 Bring healing where there is pain,
bring memories where there is emptiness.
bring hope where there is despair,
and bring love where there is hurt.

Nick Harding

12 We pray for *Name* who has died,
and for those of us who mourn and miss *her/his* company;
we pray for the grace to die a good death
and live with you for ever in the joy of heaven.

Susan Sayers

13 We remember *Name* who has come
to the end of *her/his* earthly life,
and those whose lives feel bleak
and empty without *her/him*.
We pray for mercy and peace and comfort.

Susan Sayers

14 May *Name* who has died in faith
live for ever in the joy and peace of heaven
as a child of Promise;
and may those who miss *her/his* company
be comforted and supported.

Susan Sayers

15 If I should die before the rest of you
break not a flower nor inscribe a stone;
nor when I am gone, speak in a Sunday voice,
but be the usual selves that I have known.

Weep if you must.
Parting is hell.
But life goes on.
So sing as well.

Joyce Grenfell

Prayers for the departed

16 Give rest, O Christ, to your servant with the saints:
where sorrow and pain are no more,
neither sighing, but life everlasting.
You only are immortal, the Creator and Maker of all:
and we are mortal, formed from the dust of the earth,
and unto earth shall we return.
For so you ordained when you created us saying:
'Dust you are and to dust you shall return.'
All of us go down to the dust,
Yet weeping at the grave we make our song:
Alleluia, alleluia, alleluia.
Give rest, O Christ, to your servant with the saints:
where sorrow and pain are no more,
neither sighing, but life everlasting.

Eastern Orthodox Kontakion for the Departed

17 We pray,
that *Name* who has died in faith
may rise to eternal life,
and that we may so live on earth
that we are all prepared
for meeting you face to face in heaven.

Susan Sayers

18 We remember *Name,*
who has completed *her/his* earthly life in faith
and has now seen you face to face.
May *she/he* know the peace of eternity;
we too look forward to sharing that life of joy.

Susan Sayers

19 Father, may *Name* who has died
rest in the eternal peace of your presence,
her/his burdens laid down and *her/his* suffering ended.

Susan Sayers

20 We rejoice in the risen Lord and the promise of eternal life.
Lord, bless our loved one departed.
May *she/he* share with your saints in glory.
To you and your unfailing love
we commit ourselves and the whole world
in time and for eternity.

David Adam

21 Loving God, we pray for *Name*
who has died to this earthly life,
and now sees you face to face.
We remember your mercy
and commit our loved one
to the safety of your keeping.

Susan Sayers

22 God of eternity,
we remember *Name* who, healed for ever,
lives with you in the fullness of life.
We pray that we too may come, by your grace,
to share the life which has no ending.

Susan Sayers

23 We pray for those who have died,
and particularly for those
who have no one to mourn their going;
for those who have died unnoticed.
We pray that they may rest in your peace for ever.

Susan Sayers

24 We rejoice in the fellowship of your saints
and all who have reflected your image here on earth.
We pray for our friend and loved one
who has enriched our lives
and is now departed from us.
Lord, we commit ourselves, all on earth and in heaven
to you and your unfailing love.

David Adam

25 Welcome into your kingdom
Name who has faithfully lived out *her/his* days;
as we miss *her/his* physical presence,
we thank you for the gift of *her/his* life.

Susan Sayers

26 We pray that *Name* who has wearily
struggled to death
may know the joy of burdens laid down,
and new, lasting life transforming *her/him*
through the eternal love of God.

Susan Sayers

27 As we remember with love
Name who has journeyed through physical death,
we pray that, nourished by the Bread of Life,
she/he may travel on eagles' wings
into the brightness of eternal life.

Susan Sayers

28 Father, earth-bound we grieve
at the loss of our loved one through death;
yet we also rejoice in you calling *her/him* out
into the fullness of everlasting life.

Susan Sayers

29 We give thanks for the fullness of eternal life.
We ask your blessing upon our loved ones
who have entered into the fullness of your kingdom
and all the faithful departed.
We pray for the day
when we may all see you more clearly
and walk without fear in your light.

David Adam

30 We rejoice that in you all ills come to an end
and all pain is taken away.
We give thanks for the gift of eternal life.
We give thanks for all the saints
and we remember our loved one who is departed from us.

David Adam

31 Lord, your death and resurrection
proclaim the message of hope
among the tears of our grieving
for *Name* who has died.
Welcome *her/him* into the eternal light of your kingdom.

Susan Sayers

32 We have lost someone special,
someone who was part of us,
someone who was here with us,
someone who was one of us.
We have lost someone special,
someone who made us complete,
someone who added so much.
We have lost someone special.

Nick Harding

33 Fold *her/him,* Jesus, in your arms
and let *her/him* henceforth be a messenger
between our human hearts and you.

Author unknown

Continued overleaf

34 Sleep, sleep, and away with sorrow,
sleep in the arms of Jesus.
Sleep in the calm of all calm,
sleep in the love of all loves.
Sleep heaven's life eternal.

(Echoes a prayer in the Carmina Gadelica)

Ray Simpson

35 Creator, lover of souls,
you uphold us in life and sustain us in death.
We thank you for our loved ones whom we see no longer.
as the sun goes down in the west may they now rest in you.

Ray Simpson

Prayers for ourselves

36 Lord Jesus,
you know what it's like
to lose a friend.
you know what it's like
to see your friends crying
because someone they love
has died.
Lord Jesus,
you wept
when Lazarus, your friend,
died.
You wept
when you saw his sisters,
and you shed your tears
for someone you loved,
even though you brought
Lazarus
back to life.
Lord Jesus,
thank you
that you understand how we
feel
and even though we believe
in life after death,
we know it's OK
to cry
because
you wept.

Tony Bower

37 Crucified and risen Lord
you know the grief of our hearts
the pain of our loss
the agony we share.
Have mercy upon us
in our frailty and sorrow,
and teach us that
deeper than our fears

Continued overleaf

the power of your love
is constant and abiding,
stronger than loss and death.
Nourish this faith,
we pray,
constantly within us;
and so renew in us day by day
a firm step,
a bright hope,
and in the confidence of your mercy
a joyful disposition,
that amid all the tribulations of the world
we may yet be diffusers of life;
by the power of your Spirit,
and in the name of Jesus Christ.

Patrick Woodhouse

38 Lord,
we come to you just as we are,
with no pretence, no bravery.
We lay before you our worries and our fears,
our grief, our tears,
and all the pain and confusion
of these dark days.
Please help us to carry the burden
and to bear it all,
and may your peace reign
in our hearts and lives.

Susan Hardwick

39 God of all comfort,
in the traumas and tragedies of life,
the vagaries of our ever-changing world,
speak your word,
grant your strength and minister your love,
through Jesus Christ our Lord.

Nick Fawcett

40 We pray for *Name* who has died
and those who grieve for the loss of *her/his* company.
We ask for the opportunity to prepare for death
by the way we live from now on.
We bring to mind our circle of family and friends
with whom we share the good and the difficult times.
We pray for the grace to discern more readily
the good in each person and the gifts they have to offer.

Susan Sayers

41 Living God,
where death casts its shadow over life,
seeming to block out all rays of hope,
remind us of your promised kingdom
in which there will be no more night,
nor need for lamp or sun,
for your light will be all in all,
shining for ever more.

Nick Fawcett

42 Lord Jesus Christ,
just as death could not hold you
teach us that the grave can never hold us,
for your purpose continues,
your grace persists,
and your love endures not just today but for all eternity.
In that knowledge,
teach us to live life and meet death in the same way:
in quiet confidence and firm hope,
through Jesus Christ our Lord.

Nick Fawcett

43 Living God,
teach us to recognise that death is not so much an end
as a new beginning,
leading us into fullness of life,
enduring for all eternity.

Nick Fawcett

44 O God, who brought us to birth and in whose arms we die,
in our grief and shock contain, sustain and comfort us,
embrace us with your love,
give us hope in our confusion and grace to let go.

Ray Simpson

45 Sovereign God,
instead of fearing death,
teach us eagerly to anticipate your kingdom
and the new life we will celebrate within it,
through Jesus Christ our Lord.

Nick Fawcett

46 Lord Jesus Christ,
may new life be born within us this and every day,
and may your life-giving hope sustain us
through the joys and sorrows of this world
until that time when we pass through the shadow of death
into the light of your eternal kingdom.

Nick Fawcett

47 Everlasting God,
help us to realise more and more
that time and space are not the measure of all things.
Though our eyes do not see,
teach us to understand
that the souls of our dear ones are not cut off.
Love does not die,
and truth is stronger than the grave.
Just as our affection and the memory of the good
they did
unite us with them at this time,
so may our trust in you lift us
to the vision of the life that knows no death.

God of our strength,
in our weakness help us;
in our sorrow comfort us;
in our confusion guide us.
Without you our lives are nothing;
with you there is fullness of life for ever more.

Jewish funeral prayer

48 Holy God, holy and mighty,
you alone are Creator
you alone are saviour of all
you alone are immortal.

We are mortal,
formed from the earth, returning to the earth;
for you ordained
that we should come from dust and go to dust.
Yet through Christ you ordained also
that with our tears at the dark night of parting
should be mingled the Alleluias
of the glory that pierces the gloom from beyond.
So as we remember the shadows,
and as we linger with our precious memories,
may we feel your presence.
May we be touched by your hope.
May we be changed by your glory.

Ray Simpson

49 Living God,
teach us to look beyond the apparent finality of death
to the new life you hold for all your people,
and help us to rest secure in the knowledge
that nothing can finally separate us or those we love
from your sovereign purpose in Jesus Christ our Lord.

Nick Fawcett

Continued overleaf

50 Bring us, O Lord our God, at our last awakening,
into the house and gate of heaven,
to enter into that gate and dwell in that house,
where there shall be no darkness or dazzling,
but one equal light;
no noise or silence,
but one equal music;
no fears or hopes,
but one equal possession;
no ends or beginnings,
but one equal eternity;
in the habitations of thy glory and dominion,
world without end.

John Donne (1572–1631)

51 Giver of all
from you we come,
to you we go.
May nothing unquiet mark our leaving this earth;
may nothing unquiet disturb those who have passed over.

Ray Simpson

Prayers for specific occasions

After abortion, miscarriage or stillbirth

52 Receive, Lord, this child,
taken from us so suddenly and painfully,
before love could fully be expressed,
relationships built
or dreams fulfilled,
yet nonetheless meaning so much in so many ways.
Support *parent(s) name(s)* through this time,
in all the sorrow, pain and confusion they feel,
and help them somehow to deal with their loss
and find strength and hope to face the future.

Nick Fawcett

53 **Parent** Dear God, full of a tender mother's heart, this
child who was lost was yours and mine,
and I am yours.

I wish to name before you my child
who was born on *date*.
I name *her/him* . . .
I ask you to heal *her/him* of any shock or hurt
she/he has carried as a result of the way
she/he has died.
Now I place my child into your loving care.

Minister We release *Name*
into your loving arms, O God.
Bring *her/him* to wholeness
in your eternal kingdom.

A flower, plant, plaque or cross may be placed in a place of remembrance.

Continued overleaf

The minister holds a crucifix or cross in front of the parents and says:

Minister Christ died on a cross and came back
to bring us all life.
May this cross come between you and the past.
May Christ hold you in this life
and hold *Name* in the life beyond.

May you find healing of past wounds.
May you walk free into fruitful paths.

God be with you each day of your life ahead.

Ray Simpson

54 *Parent:*
Dear God, the *child/children* who *was/were* lost through abortion are mine and yours. It helps to know that no child is lost to you.

First, I wish to say I am especially sorry that the life of my . . . (*first, or second etc.*) child was taken through abortion. I am truly sorry for the taking of this life. I ask forgiveness from you and from the child who has died. I acknowledge before you that this was truly a child and was truly my own.

A minister or friend:
We release *Name* into your hands. May your blessing and your peace be upon *Name*. Bring *her/him* to wholeness in your eternal kingdom.

Parent:
Now, dear Jesus, I wish to name before you the one who was born on (*date*). In faith I name *her/him*. I ask you to heal *Name,* too, of any shock or hurt *she/he* has carried as a result of the way *she/he* died. I place this child into your tender care. I assure *him/her* of my love.

Blessings on the parent by a soul friend or minister:
Lord Jesus, in your name we break the power of the past to have a hold over *Name* now. May the cross of Christ come between you and your past. The love of Jesus fill you, a lamb of choosing, that you may rest in his arms and walk free into the fruitful paths he has for you.

A cross, flower, plant or plaque may be placed in a place of remembrance. Three drops of water may be poured on that spot, using this prayer for a baby:

A little drop of your Creator, precious one.
A little drop of your Saviour, precious one.
A little drop of your Guardian Spirit, precious one.
To bless you with virtue and sweetness.
To keep you in eternal life.

There may be words of praise, encouragement or singing; if desired, there may be the laying on of hands in silent or spoken prayer.

Blessing:
May the tender and gracious God pour out love upon you.
May you walk free and walk tall.
May the Creator's power protect you.
The Saviour's care enfold you.
The Spirit's life renew you.
May you walk in the blessing of the Three of limitless love
now and for ever.

Ray Simpson

55 In the heartbreak of broken dreams
and shattered expectations,
the numbness of shock and disbelief,
the ache of grief and despair,
the pain of loss and bereavement,
may your love, Lord, somehow bring strength,
support,
courage
and comfort.
Receive this little one into your eternal care,
and assure us of your purpose beyond death itself,
through Jesus Christ our Lord.

Nick Fawcett

Death of a young girl

56 She stood on the brink of adulthood,
a rosebud not yet fully in bloom
and with the potential
of so much more to come.
A pre-mature flower cruelly cut from the stem.
Lord, can it really be true
she is blossoming in another place
and that one day we will see her again?
She was our darling:
no parents could have been prouder.
Thank you, Lord,
for those golden and magical years.

Susan Hardwick

Death of a pupil or teacher

57 Heavenly Father,
at present we can only feel the loss of *Name*
We want to be strong and we want to understand why
she/he is no longer here with us.
We pray that *Name* is safe in your arms, in your heavenly kingdom.
Help us to remember what *she/he* meant to us and what
she/he left behind – the laugh, the smile, the favourite comment,
the things *she/he* struggled with.
Bring us happy memories in the tears.
Bring *her/him* the peace only you can give, Lord of love
and mercy.
We ask this in Jesus' name

Rupert Bristow

58 Lord Jesus,
we are stunned at the loss of *Name*
and as a community we have gathered together
to share our sorrow, our bewilderment and our pain.
'*Why?*' is a question we're all asking,
but there seems to be no easy answer.

We pray now for *her/his* friends,
her/his classmates, *her/his* teachers
and all who knew *her/him*.
We remember *her/his* for
(*list some personality traits*)
We may not understand, Lord,
but help us to let go our bewilderment,
our anger and any desire for revenge.
May our tears be replaced by smiles
when we think of *Name*
giving thanks for *her/his* life
and all that *she/he* was to us.
Help us now to pick up the pieces once again
and to carry on.

Author unknown

59 Heavenly Father,
we give thanks for the life of *Name*; for the smiles, the fun
and the friendships *she/he* brought to our lives.
Through our tears we ask, Lord, that as *she/he* is welcomed
into your loving arms *she/he* also stays in our hearts.
She/he will always be special to *Name* school
Help us all, family, friends and community, to say farewell
to *Name* but never to forget *her/him*.
We ask this in Jesus' name

Rupert Bristow

60 Almighty God,
you know that it will be difficult for us at *Name* school
without *Name*.
Bring us the strength and the hope to carry on, as *she/he*
would have wished.
We thank you, Lord, for the special gifts *she/he* brought
to the school and shared with us.
May the church and the wider community give thanks
for *her/his* contribution to the life of *Name (village /town)*
and may we redouble our own efforts to serve each other,
in honour of *her/his* memory.
We ask this through Jesus Christ, our Lord.

Author unknown

61 Heavenly Father,
as we remember all that *Name* has meant to us at *Name* school, we pray that *she/he* is now at peace with you in your eternal kingdom.
Only you know why *she/he* was taken from us at this time, but we give thanks for *her/his* special place in our hearts at our school.
We pray for *her/his* family and friends at this difficult time.
Show your love for them and for us as we struggle to cope with the loss.
May your church be a comfort and a strength to us all.
We ask this through Jesus Christ, our Lord.

Rupert Bristow

Death by suicide, accident, violence or murder

62 After shock and trauma,
bring, Lord, your peace and blessing:
peace such as this world cannot give,
blessing beyond anything we can ever ask or imagine,
each enduring for all eternity –
nothing ever again,
in heaven or on earth,
able to hurt, destroy or overshadow your great love,
through Jesus Christ our Lord.

Nick Fawcett

63 We pray for all who have died violently
or suddenly, or with no one to miss them.
May all who have died in faith
be judged with mercy
and welcomed into eternal life.

Susan Sayers

64 Loving Father, we pray for those
who have died alone, unmourned and unnoticed.
We pray for those who have committed suicide
or died in accidents of their own making.
We commend them to your merciful love.

Susan Sayers

65 God of life,
we pray for those whose earthly lives have ended;
we remember those who have died
violently and tragically, suddenly and unprepared.
We give you thanks for lives well lived
and for happy memories.
May they rest in the eternal peace of heaven.

Susan Sayers

66 Now *she/he* is at peace in your nearer presence,
Lord,
may the misery,
the loneliness,
the pain *she/he* felt
somehow find a value.
May *her/his* suffering not be in vain.
In some deeply mystical way
may it be transformed into good.
Take it all and recreate it
in the furnace of your love.

Susan Hardwick

67 We commend to your love and mercy
all those who have made the journey
through death,
especially any who have died unprepared,
or violent deaths.
We thank you for your understanding
and compassion
and pray that they may know the forgiveness,
peace and joy of heaven.

Susan Sayers

Prayers with congregational responses

68 Loving God,
we praise you that on this day of mourning,
and at this time of pain,
we can come still with hope in our hearts
and thanksgiving on our lips,
for we know that what seems like the end
with you is a new beginning.
Christ has died.
Christ has risen.
Thanks be to God!

We praise you that in Jesus
you experienced not just our life but our death –
that you endured the darkness of Gethsemane,
the agony of the cross,
and the finality of the tomb;
and you emerged victorious,
triumphant over everything that would keep us from you,
conquering death itself.
Christ has died.
Christ has risen.
Thanks be to God!

We thank you that where the world saw only defeat
you brought victory;
that in despair and sorrow you brought joy;
that in darkness and doubt you brought light;
that nothing is able to overshadow your love,
no power able to withstand your purpose.
Christ has died.
Christ has risen.
Thanks be to God!

Loving God,
we praise you that we can come today
not to close a book but to end a chapter,
not to say goodbye
but rather to bid a friend farewell for now.
In that confidence we entrust *Name* into your eternal care,
knowing that the love which surrounds *her/him*
surrounds us all,
now and for ever more.
Christ has died.
Christ has risen.
Thanks be to God!

Nick Fawcett

69 Gracious God,
we entrust *Name* into your everlasting care,
and, as we do so, we thank you again
for all *she/he* has meant to us,
for the person *she/he* has been,
for the service *she/he* has offered
and for the contribution *she / he* has made to our lives.
Gratefully we come:
lovingly we give thanks.

We thank you for everything *Name* has meant to *her/his* family,
to colleagues and friends,
to us here today,
and we thank you for all *she/he* continues to mean to you
as well as to us.
Gratefully we come:
lovingly we give thanks.

We thank you for *Name*'s achievements
which we can look back on with pride,
the challenges faced,
the obstacles overcome,
the successes won,
the potential fulfilled.
Gratefully we come:
lovingly we give thanks.

Continued overleaf

We thank you for the experiences we have been
through together,
the love and friendship we have shared,
the qualities and characteristics which made *Name*
special to us.
Gratefully we come:
lovingly we give thanks.

We thank you for *Name*'s faith,*
her/his commitment to Christ,
faithful discipleship
and personal experience of your love.
Gratefully we come:
lovingly we give thanks.

We thank you for all we owe to *Name*,
for the innumerable ways in which *she/he* enriched our lives,
and for the memories we will always have
as a lasting tribute and enduring legacy.
Gratefully we come:
lovingly we give thanks.

Gracious God,
we come in hope and confidence,
trusting in your promise,
and assured of your gracious purpose,
and in that faith we entrust both *Name* and ourselves
into your gracious keeping,
now and for all eternity.
Gratefully we come:
lovingly we give thanks.

Through Jesus Christ our Lord.

Nick Fawcett

* Omit this stanza if the deceased professed no Christian faith

70 Loving God,
as we wrestle now with our grief,
we are reminded of all who have lost loved ones,
whose lives have been touched by tragedy,
and who are overwhelmed by sorrow.
Lord, in your mercy,
hear our prayer.
We pray for them in their shock, hurt and bewilderment.
We lift before you their sense of desolation and despair,
their feelings of numbness and emptiness,
their aching hearts which see just a blank void
where so much joy used to be.
Lord, in your mercy,
hear our prayer.

We pray for each one of us here today
and especially for those closest to *Name;*
for (*names as appropriate*).
Reach out and encircle them in your loving arms.
Grant them the comfort you have promised to all who mourn,
your peace that passes understanding,
your light that reaches into the darkest places of life
and beyond into the darkness of death.
Lord, in your mercy,
hear our prayer.

Loving God,
may the hope of the gospel,
the experience of your love
and the support of family and friends
bring the help that is needed at this time;
the strength to endure sorrow in all its intensity
and to face death in all its apparent finality,
yet ultimately to look forward in faith,
knowing that, in Christ, nothing can finally separate us
from you or from those we love.
Lord, in your mercy,
hear our prayer.

We ask it for his name's sake.

Nick Fawcett

71 Loving God,
you have promised that those who mourn shall be comforted.
So we pray now for each of us here today,
bringing before you the sorrow we all feel at this moment.
Lord, in your mercy,
hear our prayer.

We pray especially for *Name's* family,
in their shock and grief,
their pain and loneliness,
the turmoil of emotions which death inevitably brings
to those left behind.
Lord, in your mercy,
hear our prayer.

We pray for all those who counted *Name* as a friend,
those in this church,
those who worked with *Name,*
who lived near to *her/him,*
who shared *her/his* hobbies and interests –
all those whose lives were, in different ways,
touched by *Name's* presence.
Lord, in your mercy,
hear our prayer.

Loving God,
we bring before you now our sense of emptiness,
separation and sorrow.
Give us your support as we struggle
to come to terms with our loss.
Give strength to face the days ahead.
Give courage when life seems dark.
Give hope when the future seems without purpose.
Lord, in your mercy,
hear our prayer.

Help us to know that your love for *Name* and for us
continues beyond death,
that you are with us in this moment and always,
and may that knowledge bring comfort and hope
today and in the days ahead.
Lord, in your mercy,
hear our prayer,
in the name of Christ.

Nick Fawcett

72 We make our prayers now
that our *sister/brother* who has died
may find a welcome in heaven
and peace that will never be disturbed.

We pray that all the good
done by our *sister/brother* in this life
may continue to bear fruit
in our own world,
in our own lives.

Lord, in your mercy,
hear our prayer.

We pray that any hurt or harm
done in this life
may be forgiven and forgotten.
May we always remember the good things.

Lord, in your mercy,
hear our prayer.

We pray for all those who mourn
the loss of a loved one,
and the best of friends.
May we firmly believe
that we shall meet again
in a happier world.

Lord, in your mercy,
hear our prayer.

As Christ our Lord
suffered death but conquered it,
so may he bring our *sister/brother*
safely to the shores
of Paradise.

Lord, in your mercy,
hear our prayer.

Continued overleaf

May we who remain
find the courage to start again,
confident that our loss is heaven's gain,
and that all will be well in the end,
by the Providence of God.

Lord, in your mercy,
hear our prayer.

In silence for a few moments we tell God of our own feelings today.

Heavenly Father,
our hearts are restless until they find rest in you.
We pray that our *sister/brother*
may have found that rest,
through Christ our Lord.

Gerald O'Mahony

73 Gracious God,
we entrust *Name* into your everlasting care,
and, as we do so, we thank you again
for all *she/he* has meant to us,
for the person *she/he* has been,
for the service *she/he* has offered
and for the contribution *she/he* has made to our lives.
Gratefully we come:
lovingly we give thanks.

We thank you for everything *Name* has meant to *her/his* family,
to colleagues and friends,
to us here today,
and we thank you for all *she/he* continues to mean to you
as well as to us.
Gratefully we come:
lovingly we give thanks.

We thank you for *Name*'s achievements
which we can look back on with pride,
the challenges faced,
the obstacles overcome,
the successes won,
the potential fulfilled.
Gratefully we come:
lovingly we give thanks.

We thank you for the experiences we have been through together,
the love and friendship we have shared,
the qualities and characteristics which made *Name* special to us.
Gratefully we come:
lovingly we give thanks.

We thank you for *Name*'s faith*,
her/his commitment to Christ,
faithful discipleship and personal experience of your love.
Gratefully we come:
lovingly we give thanks.

We thank you for all we owe to *Name*,
for the innumerable ways in which *she/he* enriched our lives,
and for the memories we will always have
as a lasting tribute and enduring legacy.
Gratefully we come:
lovingly we give thanks.

Gracious God,
we come in hope and confidence,
trusting in your promise,
and assured of your gracious purpose,
and in that faith we entrust both *Name* and ourselves
into your gracious keeping,
now and for all eternity.
Gratefully we come:
lovingly we give thanks.

Through Jesus Christ our Lord.

* Omit this stanza if the deceased professed no Christian faith

Author unknown

74 Loving God,
you tell us to look forward to a day
when your kingdom shall come
and your will be done;
a new age when there will be no more suffering,
sorrow or death;
a place where there will be no more mourning and weeping,
every tear wiped away from our eyes.
Help us to find comfort in your love.

We thank you for that promise,
And we look forward to that time,
but we pray also for your help now,
for today our grief is all too painful,
and the fact of death an all too stark reality.
Help us to find comfort in your love.

So we ask you to reach out to us
and to all whose lives have been enriched
by *Name*'s presence –
family,
friends,
neighbours,
colleagues –
each so much the poorer for *Name*'s passing.
Help us to find comfort in your love.

Loving God,
reach out now into the darkness of this moment,
the blackness of our sorrow,
and grant your light which nothing can overcome,
your peace that defies understanding,
and your hope which will never be extinguished.
Help us to find comfort in your love,
through Jesus Christ our Lord.

Nick Fawcett

75 We make our final prayers together
here where our *sister/brother*
comes to a final rest.
We remember that each of us
is precious in God's eyes.

In baptism we were given
each our own place at God's family table.
May our friend now claim
that promised place
at the wedding feast in heaven.

Lord, in your mercy,
hear our prayer.

Our names are branded on the hands of God,
so that he never forgets a single one of us.
May he welcome his chosen one
in peace and joy.

Lord, in your mercy,
hear our prayer.

God the Good Shepherd
looks for the lost one,
searches for the stray,
binds up the wounds of the wounded ones.
We commend our *sister/brother* to his tender care.

Lord, in your mercy,
hear our prayer.

Not one sparrow falls to the ground,
but that our heavenly Father knows all about it.
How much more precious are God's children!
We commend all the lonely people,
to God who understands
and who will make all well.

Lord, in your mercy,
hear our prayer.

Continued overleaf

May we who are left behind
not be troubled any more
by the things we might have said,
the things we might have done.
May we leave all to the mercy of God.

Lord, in your mercy,
hear our prayer.

For a moment in silence we pray our own thoughts in God's presence.

God our Father,
even if a human father or mother
should ever forget their own child,
you will never forget a single one of us.
In your mercy, take to yourself
our *sister/brother* for whom we pray.
We ask this through Christ our Lord.

Gerald O'Mahony

Prayers of blessing and commendation

76 Go forth upon your journey from this world,
O Christian soul,
in the name of him in whom you have believed,
in the name of God the Father, who created you,
in the name of the Holy Spirit, who strengthened you.
May angels and archangels and the host of heaven
come to meet you.
May all the saints of God welcome you.
May your portion this day be in gladness and peace
and your dwelling in paradise.
Go forth upon your journey, O Christian soul.

Gelasian Sacramentary

77 Go forth upon your journey, Christian soul,
go from this world.
Go in the name of God, the omnipotent Father,
who created you.
Go in the name of Jesus Christ our Lord,
who died for you.
Go in the name of the Holy Spirit,
who hath been poured out on you,
and will sustain us both until we meet again.
May God be with you till we meet again.

John Henry Newman (1801–1890)

78 Go forth upon your journey from this world,
in the Name of God the Father who created you;
in the Name of Jesus Christ who died for you;
in the Name of the holy spirit who shines through you;
in friendship with God's saints;
aided by the holy angels.
May you rest this day
in the peace and love of your eternal home.

Traditional, adapted by Ray Simpson

79 Go forward on your journey, O loved child of God.
May you pass from the darkness of mortal death
into the fullness of life eternal.
May you pass from our fretful ways
into the creative peace of divine partnership.
May you pass from the knots of life and death
into the seamless tapestry of God's healing grace.

Go forth upon your journey from this world,
in the name of God the Father who created you;
in friendship with God's saints, aided by holy angels.
May you rest this day in the peace and love
of your eternal home.

Traditional, adapted

80 Go, *Name,* to your eternal home of welcome.
Go into the sleep of Jesus,
the restoring sleep of Jesus,
the young sleep of Jesus.
Go into the kiss and the peace and glory of Jesus,
into the arms of the Jesus of blessings,
into the generous Christ with his hands around you.
Draw near to the Trinity,
Freed from your pains,
Pardoned from your sins,
Christ beside you bringing peace to your mind.

May you who were baptised as *Names,*
now be immersed in the life of God.
Into the presence of the Creator I immerse you;
into the presence of the Saviour I immerse you;
into the presence of the Spirit I immerse you.

May you be as free as the wind,
as soft as sheep's wool,
as straight as an arrow,
that you may journey into the heart of God.

Ray Simpson

81 Go on your way, *Name,* to new horizons,
new life,
new beginnings.
Go with our thanks for all you have meant to us
and will continue to mean;
for all you have contributed to our lives
in ways great and small.
Go to the one who created you,
who welcomes you now
and whose arms will enfold you always.
Go in peace until we meet again
and share once more,
never again to be parted.

Author unknown

82 Father, as Lord of both time and eternity,
we commit to your keeping
Name who has died to this life;
that, freed from all pain, and forgiven,
she/he may live in the peace and joy of heaven.

Susan Sayers

83 **Committal**

Gracious God,
we commit our friend,
our loved one,
into your everlasting care,
with sorrowful hearts,
thankful hearts
and confident hearts.
Receive *Name* into your glorious kingdom,
your peace that passes understanding,
your joy that knows no bounds,
your love that is all in all;
and grant us your guidance and strength,
until we too are with Christ,
with *Name,*
and with all your people,
rejoicing in your gracious presence,
through Jesus Christ our Lord.

Nick Fawcett

84 Father, we thank you
for all who have lived your praise
and worked for the coming of your kingdom.
Receive into the joy of heaven
Name who has died in faith,
whose strong hope in the eternal God
is not disappointed, but fulfilled.

Susan Sayers

85 As *Name* whom we have known and loved
passes through the gate of death,
have mercy on *her/him,*
and receive *her/him* into the joy
of your eternal kingdom.

Susan Sayers

86 Knowing that physical death
is not the end of life,
but the beginning of a new dimension,
we recall our loved one who has died
and commend *her/him* to your eternal keeping.

Susan Sayers

87 Loving Lord,
we leave these, our prayers of remembrance,
on your altar
and we leave *Name* whom we miss in your keeping.
May *her/his* name be remembered in your house
as *her/his* memory is cherished in our hearts.

Claire Benton-Evans

88 A chapter is closed, Lord;
another just opened.
Life is over;
it is only just starting.
The day is ended;
but it has only just begun.

With grief, then, yet with gratitude,
with heavy hearts, yet filled with hope,
we entrust *Name* and ourselves
into your sure keeping,
confident that, though all else may fail,
you will not.

Nick Fawcett

89 Father, I place *Name* in your hands;
acknowledge a sheep of your own fold,
a lamb of your own flock,
a sinner of your own redeeming.
Enfold *Name* in the arms of your mercy,
in the blessed rest of everlasting peace,
and in the glorious company of the saints in light.

Traditional

90 May kindly Michael, chief of the holy angels
take charge of your beloved soul
and tenderly bring it home
to the Three of limitless love
Creator, Saviour, eternal Life-giver.

Ray Simpson

91 May the kindly angels
take charge of your beloved soul,
and tenderly bring it home
to the eternal embrace of the Three of limitless love.

Ray Simpson

92 Father, we commend to your love and mercy
Name who has died to this earthly life.
We thank you for a life well lived and love shared.
Bring *her/him* and us in our turn safely to heaven.

Susan Sayers

93 We rejoice in life
and that you give us life eternal.
Renewing and restoring God,
we remember in your presence
our loved ones departed
and ask that they may rejoice in your presence
and in the fullness of life eternal.
We commend them, the world and ourselves
to your unfailing love.

David Adam

94 Welcome into your eternity
Name who has died in faith;
may we in our turn share with *her/him*
the joy of living with you for ever.

Susan Sayers

95 We give *her/him* back to you, dear Lord,
who gave *her/him* to us.
Yet, as you did not lose *her/him* in giving,
so we have not lost *her/him* by their return.
What you gave you take not away, O Lover of souls:
for what is yours is ours also if we are yours.

And life is eternal and love is immortal,
and death is only a horizon,
and a horizon is nothing save the limit of our sight.

Lift us up, strong Son of God, that we may see further;
cleanse our eyes that we may see more clearly;
draw us closer to yourself that we may know ourselves
to be nearer to our loved ones who are with you.

And while you prepare a place for us,
prepare us also for that happy place,
that where they are and you are,
we also may be for ever more.

William Penn (1644–1718)

96 God of eternity,
in whom there is no beginning or end,
welcome into your presence *Name* who has died,
and give comfort to those
who miss *her/his* earthly company.
Give us all a greater understanding
of the new life you offer.

Susan Sayers

97 Faithful God, we place into your loving keeping
Name who has died,
knowing *her/his* dependence on you
and your limitless mercy.
We thank you for *her/him* and *her/his* gifts to the world,
and ask that we may, in our turn,
come to you across the waters of death
and live in your company for ever.

Susan Sayers

98 Heavenly Father, as real and living for the dead
as for those of us walking through time,
we commend to your mercy and love
Name who has died in your faith and friendship;
may we all share in the joy
of Christ's coming in glory.

Susan Sayers

99 Gracious God,
bringer of life out of the dust,
new life out of the ashes,
we commit *Name* and ourselves
into your loving and everlasting arms.
In life or in death,
bless us by your renewing power and restoring touch,
and lead us into your eternal kingdom,
through Jesus Christ our Lord.

Nick Fawcett

100 In your tears may God give comfort;
in your turmoil, peace;
in your darkness, light;
in your despair, hope;
in your weakness, strength;
in your fear, confidence;
in your loneliness, support;
in your pain, relief;
and at your death, life;
through Jesus Christ our Lord.

Nick Fawcett

101 We ask your blessing
upon all who have found their rest in you.
We remember our friend and loved one departed.
May *she/he* find in you rest, renewal
and the joy of the resurrection.

David Adam

102 Deep peace of the quiet earth;
deep peace of the heavenly spheres;
deep peace of the still waters;
deep peace of the Son of Peace.
Peace above all peace.
Peace without end.

Irish blessing

103 God be with you today and for ever;
Jesus be in you to pardon and tether;
Spirit be on you and leave you never.

Ray Simpson

104 Blessing during the interment of ashes

God's blessing be upon you, *Name*,
for everything you have meant and will always mean.
Bless you for happiness shared:
laughter, pleasure, jubilation;
for occasions shared:
holidays, anniversaries, celebrations;
for difficulties shared:
disappointments, problems, crises;
for closeness shared:
love, friendship, commitment.
For all we have gone through together,
and all we will share in life to come,
God's blessing be upon you.

Nick Fawcett

105 Blessing during the scattering of ashes

Lord of life,
for all this place meant to *Name*, we thank you,
for all *Name* meant to us, we praise you,
for all *she/he* will always mean in our hearts,
we acknowledge you,
for all *she/he* means still to you, we worship you.
We return *Name* to you,
remembering that, though we scatter now these ashes
in fond farewell,
your love lives on and purpose continues.
Bless *Name*,
bless us,
through Jesus Christ our Lord.

Author unknown

Dedication of plaque, stone or memorial

106 Loving God,
we dedicate this *plaque / stone / memorial* to *Full Name*
in the name of Christ,
as a symbol of our remembering,
a sign of our thanksgiving,
a token of our recognition
and an expression of our love.
We look back with gratitude for all *Name* has meant to us,
for everything we have shared together,
for *her/his* love as a *husband / wife/,*
parent/, brother / sister/, friend,
for all the things which made *her/him*
such a special part of our lives.

We look forward in confidence,
in faith,
and in expectation
to our reunion with *Name,*
with all your people,
and with Christ himself,
in your everlasting kingdom;
that time when there will be no more pain,
and no more tears,
an end to suffering, sin and death.

And so we pray for your continued comfort in the present,
your strength and support,
your peace and guidance,
your help to laugh and love once more.
May we honour *Name* by honouring you
and living each day to your praise and glory,
through Jesus Christ our Lord.

Nick Fawcett

Thoughts and Reflections

Reflections on death and grief by Susan Hardwick

107 Death

Whether the death of a loved one is anticipated and prepared for or unexpected and sudden, the actual moment of its happening is usually devastating. However foreseen, nothing can prepare those closest for the feelings they experience. Numbness; shock; disbelief; deep grief; anger at God, the doctors and nurses, or at the injustice of it all; feelings of guilt for what was not done for the deceased; denial; relief that he or she is finally out of pain; these are just some of the very usual feelings expressed at the time of death, and after.

They do not happen in any neat order or pattern, for we will each react in our individual and unique way. We have to be gentle with ourselves at this time, giving ourselves permission for these turbulent feelings, which will most probably repeat themselves many times over the succeeding weeks and months, and maybe even years, before we can declare ourselves truly healed.

108 Miscarriage

Until the last few years, there was little understanding – except by those who had experienced it themselves – of the great emotional distress caused by miscarriage. However, whereas fomerly, once the physical effects of the miscarriage were over, the woman concerned was expected to carry on as normal, now there is a much greater understanding of the mental and emotional trauma involved for both the mother and the father.

The reality of that little life is now much more often acknowledged and, when possible and appropriate, the foetus is wrapped in a shawl and given to the parent(s) to hold and to cuddle. They are encouraged to name the child, thereby giving it an identity and status – no longer 'it' but 'him' or 'her' – and from there on to see that life as an acknowledged part of their family: their first, second, or whichever, child.

If wished, photos may be taken of them holding the baby. When enough time has been given to them for this process, they are encouraged to bid farewell to their baby, allowing the moment to speak to them as it will.

All this allows the grieving process to be healthily facilitated, rather than being buried only to resurrect itself at some future time and place, often seemingly quite unconnected with the event.

109 Abortion

The motives for choosing to have an abortion for non-medical reasons can be many and complex, and the decision is not usually taken lightly. All sorts of consideration will most likely have been taken into account before the mother-to-be and her partner reach what might have been an agonising choice for them.

In recent years, the whole subject of abortion has had a very high profile, with the pro-life and freedom of choice movements representing opposite views.

As Christians, we might well have clearly thought-out views about the ethics and morals of a choice for abortion. However, as pastoral carers, we need also to be able to step outside our own emotional involvement and to lay aside our own particular feelings and conclusions – whatever they may be – in order to help those who come to us for advice or comfort or both. We need to do this in order to be able to help them verbalise their own feelings of, maybe, uncertainty or confusion, fear, anguish or guilt; to help them work through the reasons for such a proposed course of action and to reach a prayerful decision which is right for them and the unborn child, and then to minister God's healing and grace at the heart of any pain and guilt.

If such situations are not handled sensitively, and any guilt and pain are pushed 'underground', it may be years before those feelings find their way once more to the surface, often triggered by some seemingly totally unconcerned event and quite likely displaced on to something or someone else, and having increased greatly in force.

110 Termination

On occasion, when the foetus has died in the mother's womb but she has not miscarried spontaneously, or when the mother's life is threatened by the pregnancy for some reason, the pregnancy has to be terminated. Usually, drugs are given that cause the uterus to contract and to expel the foetus. This distressing and often frightening experience takes place in a hospital or at home, depending upon a number of factors such as how advanced the pregnancy is. Larger hospitals have special termination units, where the staff are experienced in dealing sensitively with such patients, and where the mother does not have her distress compounded by being with other mothers who are not experiencing complications and the sight and sound of whose babies crying only serves to emphasise the loss. However, smaller hospitals usually do not have enough demand to set aside such facilities, and the mother has to be treated in the general maternity unit. Although the staff try to separate mothers going through termination from the other women, it is obviously difficult.

111 Death of a child

Of all bereavements, the death of one's child must be one of the worst.

It shouts against all that one expects; against the perceived proper order of things. Added to the parents' devastating grief, often, are anguished imaginings that their child is 'out there somewhere', wandering scared, alone and lonely, crying for the parents who are unable to be there for them to comfort, to protect and to reassure.

Perhaps only another mother can know how particularly a mother suffers when her child suffers, the child whom she has carried in her womb and given birth to; how she would do anything, bear anything, in order to take away her child's suffering and pain. However, it is important we remember that the father also suffers acutely and, in addressing the needs of the mother, his needs should not be forgotten. The stiff upper lip tradition, 'boys don't cry', the expectation that the man will support the woman, all kinds of social and gender stereotypes, can bring great suffering to a bereaved father.

Bereaved parents, years after the child's death, often speak of their longing to die and to be with their child – even if they have other, living offspring. This can give rise to dismay and guilt that they are denying the gift of their own life and the value of their other children by feeling this way, and so they may need reassurance on these occasions that such ambivalent feelings are quite natural and normal.

Although each child is loved uniquely, the loss of an only child is particularly traumatic, for a whole world of identity is lost. The couple are no longer parents, with all that involves socially and in the wider community. On an immediate day-to-day basis, huge areas of social contact disappear. No more gathering at the school gate, taking one's turn with other parents ferrying children, and so on. Added to all of this are often guilt-loaded feelings of why it could not have happened to someone with several children.

112 Death by violence: suicide or murder

It is difficult enough to face, to cope and to come to terms with the death of a loved one when the cause is accident or illness.

When the anguish of a loss is compounded by the knowledge that the life was taken deliberately – by the person who has died, or at the hands of another – extra dimensions are added to the sufferings of the bereaved which are so great as to defy description.

Surely the most dreadful type of death to face is that of murder, surrounded as it is these days by often prurient and intrusive press and media interest; by the necessary police inquiries with the constant reliving of details of the last movements of the deceased; with the dreadful imaginings of how the deceased must have suffered in their last moments. Thinking of their terror and pain, we face the knowledge that we were not there at the very moments in their life when they most needed us.

The parent(s) of a murdered child will feel the last particularly acutely: it is every parent's worst nightmare. It is hard enough when one's child is ill or in pain and all we can do is sit alongside, comfort and reassure, and surround that child with our love. To have been unable to do that at the time of their most desperate need must be almost insupportable, giving rise to the deepest anguish and guilt.

As pastoral carers we come empty handed to such situations, but with hearts brimming over with compassion, fellow suffering and God's love, meeting with the cross of Christ planted firmly at the heart of suffering.

113 Religious beliefs

Certain religious beliefs held by the bereaved may have taught them that the taking of one's own life puts that person outside the possibility of eternal redemption. Whereas normally the bereaved with a faith in the afterlife would find comfort in the notion that the parting is but a temporary one, in this situation that now no longer applies so far as they are concerned and believe.

Contemplating that the loved one is condemned to eternal damnation – whatever that may mean to them – not surprisingly gives rise to the deepest distress.

114 Guilt

There are often the deepest feelings of guilt that signs were not recognised or, if noticed, were not acted upon sufficiently. The 'if only…' path is not one to persue for too long. It is a useful tool to enable the bereaved to ventilate their feelings of guilt, but then it is wise to gently help them understand that, almost certainly, it was a whole multitude of circumstances – many of them probably quite beyond their control – that contributed to making life intolerable for the person who has died, and so they may not continue to punish themselves in this way. It will not bring the deceased back, and the bereaved will need all their inner resources to cope with the consequences of the death, both for themselves and for any others affected who may be looking to them for comfort, support and strength, such as children.

S. H.

Continued overleaf

115 A wake

The Irish wake, at which friends and family gather together round the coffin for food and music and recounting of memories, retains the Celtic idea of celebrating a life.

It can be a healing experience to keep the dead person's body in a place where friends and family can see it, sit by it, and place flowers or mementos. Some people will wish to be silent, others might wish to say a blessing such as this:

Go to your eternal home of welcome, my loved companion.
  Go into the sleep of Jesus,
  the restoring sleep of Jesus,
  the young sleep of Jesus.
Go into the kiss and the peace and glory of Jesus,
  into the arms of the Jesus of blessings,
  into the generous Christ with his hands around you;
  drawing near to the Trinity,
  freed from your pains,
  pardoned from your sins,
Christ beside you bringing peace to your mind.
  Wake-time, sorrow-sharing time.
  Wake-time, story-telling time.
  Wake-time, vigil-keeping time.
  Wake-time, embracing time.

Reflection: Ray Simpson. Poem: William J. Fitzgerald

Private Prayers

General Occasions

Loss and loneliness

116 I've lost one whom I loved, Lord,
more precious than can be,
who brought life joy and meaning,
and meant the world to me.
Each day I yearn for comfort,
yet cannot find relief –
the smile I wear in public,
a mask to hide my grief –
for all we shared is over,
its joy beyond recall;
a cloud obscures my vision
and overshadows all.
And yet, in scattered moments,
I glimpse another side –
although for now we're parted,
not everything has died:
the empathy between us,
the love that freely flowed,
the happiness and laughter,
the time and care bestowed,
all these have helped to bring me
to where I am today,
each one a priceless treasure
that death can't pluck away.
So when I'm feeling wretched,
dejected and bereft,
Lord, help me to remember
how much there still is left;
to recognise more fully
the blessings I've enjoyed:
their legacy continues
and will not be destroyed.

Nick Fawcett

117 There's so much I wanted to say, Lord,
so much I wanted to do,
all kinds of hopes left unrealised,
dreams that I'll never see through:
news I would once have related,
deeds showing how much I cared,
love I intend to speak of –
all can no longer be shared.
Help me to face my emotions,
deal with the sorrow I feel,
cope with the pain of remembering,
such that, in time, these might heal.
Teach me to look back with gladness,
happy in spite of the tears,
grateful for wonderful memories,
joy spanning so many years.
So may I find consolation
when I feel lost and alone,
able to grieve with a smile,
thankful for all I have known.

Nick Fawcett

118 Everything seems diminished,
so much no longer applies;
part of my life feels finished –
death has exacted its prize.
No more will words be spoken,
moments together be shared,
the golden thread is broken
and never can be repaired.
Come, Lord, and grant your healing,
foster contentment anew.
Reach out in love, revealing
all that in time you will do.
Though I may feel forsaken,
bleak though the world might appear,
teach me that I am mistaken –
show me I've nothing to fear.

Yes, something is completed,
but not as so many assume:
death is destroyed, defeated,
Life will burst fresh from the tomb!

Nick Fawcett

119 I thought that I was ready,
prepared to say goodbye,
aware death waits for no one;
that each of us must die,
I knew loss would be painful,
whatever time it came;
that life from that point onwards
would never feel the same,
but even though I feared it,
deep down I dared to hope
that when bereavement hit me
I'd confidently cope.

How different, Lord, the truth
now I'm facing it for real,
how deep the sense of heartbreak
and hopelessness I feel,
how bittersweet the memories,
how bleak the future seems,
how futile all my hoping
and fragile all my dreams.
A world which seemed so stable
now whirls in disarray,
for part of me is missing,
for ever plucked away.

Lord, meet me in my sorrow
and grant the help I crave,
remind me of your promise
of life beyond the grave.
Speak of your loving purpose
and help me as I grieve,
to hear your words of comfort
and truly to believe.

Nick Fawcett

120 'Rejoice in the Lord always' –
isn't that what we're told to do?
'Give thanks in all circumstances.'
'Make music in your hearts.'
And that's what I've done, Lord –
most of the time, anyway –
life being good to me,
with so much to celebrate,
so many reasons to give you thanks.
But now it's different,
for I've come face to face with sorrow,
grief no longer being about others but about me.
I've felt the agony of loss,
the pain of separation,
and where flowers once bloomed
life has become a desert.
I've tasted the gall of loneliness,
the bitterness of tears,
and where wine once flowed
now there is only vinegar.
It's been hard to praise you through that, Lord,
to sing a new song,
to make a joyful noise,
for I've been heavy within,
the sparkle gone not just from life but from faith.
Yet even there, in the darkness, I have glimpsed your face,
your hand leading me through,
and I realise now, as light beckons once more,
that you were there with me all along,
as you are with me always,
bearing my sorrow,
sharing my pain,
not expecting me to laugh through the tears
but gently wiping them away,
easing the hurt and bandaging up my wounds.
Lord, for your faithfulness even in the darkest moments,
your love that will not let me go,
receive my glad thanksgiving,
in the name of Christ.

Nick Fawcett

121 **Hold my hand**

Hold my hand, Lord.
Walk me through the loneliness
and the valley of my sorrow.
Hold on to me when I'm too afraid
to think about tomorrow.
Let me lean on you, Lord,
when I'm too weary to go on.
Hold my hand, Lord, through the night
until I see the light of dawn.

Author unknown

Anger and pain

122 How can I cope with this pain inside,
this ache within my heart?
How can I deal with the tears I hide?
Where can I even start?
When will despair loose its stranglehold
and let me find some peace?
When will I laugh as I did of old?
When will the hurting cease?
Part of my life is a part no more,
suddenly gone for good.
Nothing can be as it was before,
much though I wish it could.
Strengthen me, Lord, in this time of need,
comfort me as I mourn.
Reach out your hand to support and lead;
after the night bring dawn.

Author unknown

123 Dear God,
Please help me.
This awful pain is impossible to bear.

Susan Hardwick

124 'Lord, save me!' I cried .
'Protect me!'
'Deliver me!'
But disaster struck nonetheless,
bringing heartbreak,
hurt,
confusion.
'Lord, bring healing!' I begged.
'Bring wholeness!'
'Make well!'
But there was no happy ending,
no sudden and miraculous recovery –
just the harrowing and lingering death
of one I loved.

And I threw up my hands in anger,
asking 'Why?'
'How?'
'Where was God when I needed him?'
It shook me to the core,
my faith buckling,
all but broken,
until I remembered that those words,
'rescue us from evil',
were spoken by your Son
who went on to face evil at its fiercest,
suffering and sorrow as great as anyone's,
and I realised that the brokenness of this world
grieves you as much as me.
You were there all along, sharing the hurt,
weeping over everything that denies your love
and frustrates your purpose,
but you were there also to support and strengthen,
reaching through the pain to share it and bear it,
and finally to lead us through.
Remind me of that when life is hard
and days are dark,
and teach me, then above all times,
to pray from the heart:
'rescue me from evil'.

Nick Fawcett

125 Lord, I scarcely dare to face
the pain I feel inside,
running rather from the truth
that the one I love has died.
Though I know I need to grieve
before the wounds can heal,
I'm afraid of letting loose
the sense of loss I feel –
scared that I'll be overwhelmed,
engulfed and swept along,
the pent-up tide too fierce to stem,
the memories too strong.

Continued overleaf

Teach me, Lord, to open up
and bring my fears to you,
trusting you will still the storm
and help me work them through.
So, in time, may I look back
with thanks across the years,
thinking of the days I shared
with joy instead of tears;
confident that though, for now,
death forces us apart,
those I love are with me still,
alive within my heart.

Nick Fawcett

126 Loving Saviour,
I come to you just as I am,
with no pretence, no bravery.
I lay before you my grief and my tears,
my worries, my fears and all the confusion
and pain of these dark days.
Please help me to carry the burden
and to bear it all.
May your peace reign in my heart and my life.

Susan Hardwick

The pleasure and the pain

127 Lord, help me to remember
the person that I knew,
not some idealised portrait
no longer ringing true.
Remind me of each aspect,
the special and mundane,
the failings and the virtues,
the beautiful and plain;
the triumphs and the failures,
the happy and the sad,
the folly and the wisdom,
the good times and the bad;
the moments of contentment
and days of dark despair,
the words that spoke of anger
and deeds that spoke of care;
the laughter and the sorrow,
the pleasure and the pain,
the hopes that found fulfilment,
the dreams that proved in vain.
Not every trait was perfect,
nor every feature good,
not everything between us
worked out quite as it should,
but all these points together
combined in such a way
to craft one far more precious
than words can ever say –
a person whom I value
for everything they've been,
and one I'll go on loving
for what they'll always mean.

Nick Fawcett

128 In the sorrow that I'm feeling
as I try to take things in;
though my broken heart is reeling,
and my mind is in a spin;
call to mind, Lord, all the pleasure
that I've shared across the years –
moments I will always treasure
with a smile as well as tears:
hands that nurtured and provided,
bandaged wounds and helped me grow;
words that comforted and guided,
teaching much of what I know;
times of happiness and of laughter,
deeds that spoke of love and care,
days that I'll recall long after –
such a privilege to share.
Lord, although a weight of sadness
leaves me grieving and distressed,
deep within there's also gladness
for I've been so richly blessed.

Nick Fawcett

129 I couldn't understand, Lord
how you could let it be.
Despite my search for answers,
I simply couldn't see.
Why do we have to suffer?
Why do you let us die?
Why does so much deny you
and give your love the lie?
I've wrestled with such questions
and still not worked them out,
the best that I can offer:
a blend of faith and doubt.
Yet in this combination,
this balance of the two,
I'm coming, Lord, to wonder
if there you give a clue.

For just as talk of darkness
demands we speak of light,
so there can be no morning
unless there's also night,
no laughter without sorrow,
no pleasure without pain,
no goodness without evil,
no sunshine without rain.
Unless we have the second
we cannot have the first;
the 'best' has little meaning
unless there is a 'worst'.
Is that what you are saying
as now I grieve in turn?
Is this the vital lesson
you're asking me to learn?
Beginnings go with endings –
I've loved and I have lost.
I've shared such special blessing –
now I must bear the cost.

Nick Fawcett

The funeral

130 Dear God,
the funeral day is here.
The cars are waiting, but I am reluctant to go
to that final goodbye.
Jesus, stay very close.
Give me the strength I need to get through it.

Susan Hardwick

131 Jesus,
please give me the strength to face the day
and all whom I shall meet
with a calm spirit;
to look and to see with your eyes.
When people stumble out their sympathy
may I listen with your ears,
and may I have the grace to remember
that they might need comforting, too.
Help me to tread gently through my world today –
your world – and please will you walk beside me?

Susan Hardwick

132 The time had come, a time to die –
with heavy heart I said goodbye.
The world felt bleak, my mind was numb,
for what I feared to see had come.
Someone so dear was dead and gone,
yet, Lord, through you, life carries on –
I don't know how, I don't know when,
but, by your grace, we'll meet again.

Nick Fawcett

Trust

133 I do not know what heaven is,
the where or when or how;
if it's a kingdom yet to come
or all around us now.
I cannot claim to understand
the complex ins and outs –
in fact, along with faith I have
a healthy share of doubts.
So am I whistling in the dark,
just clutching hold of straws,
content to cling to anything
that soothes and reassures?
Is dread of facing up to truth
the root of my belief;
this hope of mine some cosy way
of coping with my grief?
It's true I'll never prove that life
continues after death,
to claim that it is otherwise
is just a waste of breath.
That one day we will rise again,
not simply turn to dust,
cannot be shown by argument,
but has to rest on trust.
Our faith in what God holds in store
goes deeper than the mind,
not solely based on reasoning
but of another kind:
its source the one who died, yet lives
and walks with us each day,
whose gracious love encircles all
each step along the way.
In him I find a certainty
on which I can depend,
for love like this, so full, so free,
can surely never end.

Nick Fawcett

134 'Happy are those who weep', you said;
happy are they who mourn –
weeping will turn to joy instead,
pleasure will be reborn;
death will not have the final word,
darkness not win the day,
laughter will once again be heard,
tears will be wiped away.
Help me to trust, Lord, though I grieve,
show me your word is true.
Give me the courage to believe
joy still can shoot anew.
Comfort me in the pain I feel,
order the storm to cease,
reach out in love to help and heal,
come now, and grant your peace.

Nick Fawcett

The future

135 Give me greater faith, Lord,
in your love that conquers death,
a love that keeps on burning
beyond our dying breath,
a purpose that continues
unchanged for ever more,
and when this life is over
still holds the best in store.
Speak of the special future
you want us to enjoy,
the blessings of your kingdom
that nothing can destroy;
a realm of awesome beauty
where joy will never cease,
no hatred there or warfare,
but everlasting peace;
a place of hope and healing
where tears are washed away,
and those oppressed by darkness
will bask in endless day.
Although my heart is heavy,
although I need to grieve,
Lord, nurture trust within me
and help me to believe.
Remind me truth is greater
than I can comprehend:
however much it seems so,
the grave is not the end.

Nick Fawcett

136 Speak of your awesome care, Lord,
that death cannot deny,
your sovereign grace and purpose,
your love that will not die.
Comfort me in my sorrow,
breathe peace within my heart,
remind me of the treasures
you promise to impart:
eternal peace and blessing,
unutterable joy,
contentment and fulfilment
that nothing can destroy.
Remind me, when I need it,
that all is yet not done –
a chapter may be over,
but life has just begun.

Nick Fawcett

137 As you were before me, at my life's beginning,
be so again, at my journey's end.

As you were beside me, at my soul's shaping,
Father, be there with me, at my journey's close.

Celtic

138 Lord,
as I rise from the dark dead time of bereavement,
help me to live the years left fully, until the day comes
for me to face my own death
in the sure and certain hope of resurrection to eternal life,
and that I shall be coming home to you:
my Saviour, my Redeemer, my Lord.

Susan Hardwick

139 Lord, autumn leaves are falling,
The trees will soon be bare;
a multitude of endings
surround me everywhere.
So much that bloomed so brightly
now seems a world away,
its glory but a memory,
supplanted by decay.
Yet hidden in the darkness,
beneath the silent earth,
already shoots are forming –
a promise of new birth.
And, softly, you are saying,
to those with ears to hear,
though death for now brings sorrow,
keep hope and do not fear.
Yes, life may seem extinguished,
but days to come will bring
beginnings after endings,
in place of winter, spring.

Nick Fawcett

140 A conversation – pain and comfort

Pain

I still can't believe it, Lord –
to think that after all we shared together,
everything we went through,
I will never see *her/him* again.
It doesn't seem possible,
for *she/he* was always so full of life,
brimming over with happiness,
bubbling with enthusiasm.
Yet there's no denying it,
for I saw *her/him* lying there,
the body cold,
the life gone.
It's over Lord, I realise that,
but it all seems so unreal,
like some ghastly dream,
some grotesque joke;
and although my mind accepts what's happened,
my heart says otherwise:
still listening for the sound of *her/his* voice,
still longing for the touch of *her/his* hand,
still searching for a glimpse of *her/his* face.
It will pass, so they tell me –
in time the wounds will heal
and the dull ache start to ease.
One day I will look at *her/his* photograph
not with numbness but with thanksgiving;
I will speak *her/his* name
not with tears of sorrow but tears of joy;
and I will look back remembering all that was
instead of all that might have been.
So at least they tell me, Lord,
and I know they mean well –
after all, life must go on.
Yet I don't want it to, not any more,
for I'm alone now,
my loved one plucked from me –
and I still can't believe it.

Comfort

My child, what can I say?
For I know no words can ease your pain,
or fill the emptiness.
But you're not alone,
for I am with you in the darkness,
reaching out to touch your bruised
and battered soul.
It hurts – of course it does –
and it will go on hurting, desperately,
day after day,
year after year,
until your final breath.
You'll never forget,
and never lose that sense of emptiness within,
for you have lost someone precious,
unique and irreplaceable in your life,
and not even time can smooth such pain away.
The wound may heal a little,
the scar become less livid,
but it will always be with you –
the price of joy,
the cost of love.
Yet I promise you this –
if you can greet your grief openly,
not letting it fester but meeting it face to face,
then you will find comfort,
rest for your soul;
and, along with that, hope,
rising like a phoenix from the ashes,
stronger and deeper
than any you have known before –
a hope able to smile through the tears
and weep through the laughter,
knowing that I am there in both.
Believe me, my child, the time will come
when you will meet your loved one again,
united with *her/him* and me and all my people
in a new and glorious kingdom,
where there will be no more pain or sorrow,
no more tears or darkness,
but life in all its fullness,
life which will never end.

Nick Fawcett

Private Prayers

Specific Occasions

Prenatal death

141 **Emptiness**

Oh Lord, I am so empty.
No one is moving inside.
And this world is hugely empty.
You know I have tried
searching and calling.
But there is no bright side.
I am without life within;
of my baby not an echo.
I am without joy without.
I am carrying shadow.
Early morning, waking,
I am the world's widow.
I am feeling for the way
to fill up, carry on,
now my alive and kicking
meaning is gone.
Still now, I am waiting for stirring;
some tiny wriggle in the advent of nothing.

Lucy Berry

142 **It's *so* unjust**

Oh, God!
I feel so *angry*,
and full of jealousy.
It's so unjust.
Others are still pregnant
– but I'm not.
Help me!

Susan Hardwick

Death of a baby

143 The hardest thing in the world

Lord,
in was the hardest thing
in the world
to cradle *her/him*
and then to hand *her/him* back,
knowing I'll never
hold *her/him* again.
Take away the ache
from my empty arms,
my empty heart.

Susan Hardwick

144 Just a few short moments

Father,
Name; your most precious gift.
So much longed for.
So very little with us.
A few short moments
which have changed us for ever.
Thank you.

Susan Hardwick

145 No chance to get to know my child

Oh, Lord,
such bright hopes
dashed so soon
with no chance
to get to know *her/him*.
What would my child
have been like?
What colour eyes and hair?
What kind of nature?

Continued overleaf

Boisterous and noisy,
or thoughtful and quiet?
Now I'll never have the answer
to my questions.
Jesus,
heal this terrible longing
and heartache.

Susan Hardwick

146 Help us to forgive you, God

Dear God!
It seems that you gave *her/him*
only to take *her/him* back.
It just seems so cruel and capricious.
Yet, in our calmer moments,
we know this is not true
and that we are blaming you
unjustly for our awful pain.
We need to put the anguish somewhere
and only you can bear it for us.
Open our minds and hearts.
Help us to understand.

Susan Hardwick

147 Jesus, hold us in our darkest hour

Lord,
when our child was born
we held *her/him* in our arms
and wondered at that new life.
Then we held *her/him* in our arms
and wondered why *she/he* should die.
Now all we can do
is hold *her/him* in our hearts.
Ours for such a very short while,
nevertheless now forever
enshrined and adored.
Jesus, hold us in your arms
in this, our darkest hour.

Susan Hardwick

Death of a young child

148 We give our child back to you, Lord

Lord,
you gave us *Name*,
to love and to cherish.
This we have done.
No one could have
adored *her/him* more.
She/he was our truly beloved.
Now we give *her/him*
back into your care.

Susan Hardwick

149 Lighten our darkness

Jesus,
most gentle and tender
friend of children.
You who valued 'the little ones
as those to whom the
kingdom of God belongs'. *
You will understand how *Name*
brought the touch of heaven
into our daily lives.
She/he transformed everything
and lit us up.
Darkness has come upon us
now that *she/he* is gone.
Lighten our darkness now
we beseech you, O Lord.

* Luke 18:16
Susan Hardwick

150 Father,
why someone so young?
Why not
one of us older ones instead?
Please help us
to understand
and to trust in you,
in this darkest of times.

Susan Hardwick

151 **The journey back to God is short**

Jesus,
Name, did not travel
far into this life,
and so did not
have far to travel
back to you.
Hold *her/him* in peace
now and for ever
in your ever-loving arms.

Susan Hardwick

Death of a young person

152 Lord,
scarcely into young adulthood:
dreams just turning into concrete reality.
One day here and so vibrant and alive,
loving and laughing – the next day gone
and leaving a gap as wide as the world
in our hearts and in our lives.
Dear God,
what is the point and the purpose
of such a terrible waste?
Please help us to understand
and to bear with this emptiness and pain.

Author unknown

Death of a sibling

153 It's so weird, Jesus –
there's only me now.
It feels as if half of me died too.
and that I've got to be
both of us to Mum and Dad.
It's really lonely, too.
I miss *her/him* so much.
Stay close.
Please.

Jesus,
I feel really guilty.
We argued so much
and I teased *her/him* so.
I loved *her/him* really
– you know that, don't you –
and I miss *her/him* heaps.
Please give *her/him* my love
– and tell *her/him* I didn't mean
the silly and unkind things
I said and did.

Susan Hardwick

Suicide

154 Dear God!
How *could she/he* do it
– to *herself/himself,*
– to me, the family?
I feel so guilty I didn't read the signs:
– though, *were* there any?
I've racked my mind for clues
I may have missed.
She/he was quiet, preoccupied:
but that was all.
Why did *she/he* suffer alone
– and then leave me to do the same?
Lord, help me!

Susan Hardwick

155 Cry of a parent

From the depths of our despair
we cry out to you, Lord.
Why couldn't we have been there
in the hour of *her/his* most desperate need?
In our most awful imaginings
we try to picture it all
her/his terror, *her/his* loneliness, *her/his* pain:
and we are torn apart.
Yet our pain links us to *her/him*
and to *her/his* suffering;
because of this, it is precious to us.
We just ask
that you will share our suffering
as we know you shared *her/his*.

Author unknown

156 Why couldn't *she/he* share her anguish?
We are *her/his* parents.
Did *she/he* think we wouldn't believe *her/him,*
wouldn't understand?
Dear God!
We feel *such* a failure:
that it was our fault.
When we think of *her/his* isolation
her/his fear, *her/his* pain,
we simply cannot bear it.
That precious life,
embodying so much potential;
how very much *she/he* was loved
and how terribly we will miss *her/him.*
Oh Jesus!
Help us cope with this unbearable pain.

Susan Hardwick

Murder

157 **Worse than animals**

In my very worst nightmares
I did not dream of this.
How could they do it?
Are they animals?
Yet animals kill only of necessity
and not from evil intent.
Now they are destroying me too
with all that I feel.
Help me!
Dear God – don't let them succeed.
Help me.

Susan Hardwick

158 **Vengeance belongs to you, not me, Lord**

Lord,
you have said vengeance belongs to you.
So help me now to hand over
terrible desire for revenge,
the hate, the pain;
all that has been tearing me in two
and driving me insane.
For your name's sake.

Author unknown

Words of comfort

159 Goodness is stronger than evil;
love is stronger than hate;
light is stronger than darkness;
life is stronger than death;
victory is ours through him who loved us.

Desmond Tutu

160 Farewell

When day is done,
a figure turns and says a last goodbye.
We cannot understand where they must go, or why.
But as they leave our sorrow
and our sad tears far behind,
they move ahead to seek the peace
that every soul must find.
For now they sail a different ship
upon a different sea –
a voyage filled with love and hope
and new discovery.
And when the journey brings them
to that distant lighted shore,
they'll be greeted
by the outstretched arms
of those who've gone before:
people they have known and loved,
and voices from the past
will be singing out the welcome news
that they are home at last.

Author unknown

161 Death is not extinguishing the light.
It is putting out the lamp because
the dawn has come.

Rabindranath Tagore

162 I am standing on the seashore.
A ship in the bay hits anchor,
spreads her white sails to the morning breeze
and starts out upon the ocean.
She is an object of beauty and strength,
and I stand and watch until she hangs
like a speck of white cloud
just where the sea and sky mingle with each other.
Then someone at my side says,
'There, she's gone!'
Gone where?
Gone from sight, that is all.
Just at that moment there are other eyes
watching her coming
and other souls taking up the glad shout,
'There, she's coming!'
And that is dying.

Author unknown

163 Those who live in the Lord never
see each other for the last time.

Author unknown

164 God be with you in your sorrow
through the night and through the day;
may some blessing come tomorrow
that will clear its cloud away.

God is generous in his giving,
give him now the soul that's fled:
may he bless with strength the living,
rest eternally the dead.

Author unknown

165 My beloved,
these moments of sadness
are ones that I share with you.
My heart aches as yours.
How I long for you to know
the depth of my love for you at this time.
It is never easy to lose
that which is precious to you.
It is not easy to say goodbye
before one is ready.

Let me ease
these moments and comfort you.
I long to touch you
with the peace of my love.
Rest your weariness in me,
for I long to bear this burden for you.
Come, draw near to me.
Your heavenly Father.

Author unknown

166 **Death is nothing at all**

Death is nothing at all.
I have only slipped away in to the next room.
I am I, and you are you.
Whatever we were to each other,
that we still are.

Call me by my old familiar name,
speak to me in the easy way
which you always used.

Put no difference in your tone,
wear no forced air of solemnity or sorrow.
Laugh as we always laughed
at the little jokes we enjoyed together.

Let my name be ever the household word
that it always was,
let it be spoken without effect,
without the trace of a shadow on it.

Continued overleaf

Life means all that it ever meant.
It is the same as it ever was;
there is unbroken continuity.

Why should I be out of mind
because I am out of sight?

I am waiting for you,
for an interval,
somewhere very near,
just around the corner.

All is well.

Henry Scott Holland